Collins

Primary Social Studies for Antigua and Barbuda

**WORKBOOK
GRADE 4**

Anthea S Thomas

William Collins' dream of knowledge for all began with the publication of his first book in 1819.

A self-educated mill worker, he not only enriched millions of lives, but also founded a flourishing publishing house. Today, staying true to this spirit, Collins books are packed with inspiration, innovation and practical expertise. They place you at the centre of a world of possibility and give you exactly what you need to explore it.

Collins. Freedom to teach.

Published by Collins
An imprint of HarperCollins*Publishers*
The News Building
1 London Bridge Street
London
SE1 9GF

HarperCollins Publishers
Macken House, 39/40 Mayor Street Upper,
Dublin 1, D01 C9W8, Ireland

Browse the complete Collins catalogue at
www.collins.co.uk

© HarperCollins*Publishers* Limited 2019
Maps © Collins Bartholomew Limited 2019, unless otherwise stated

10 9 8 7 6

ISBN 978-0-00-832496-4

All rights reserved. No part of this publication may be reproduced, stored in a retrieval system, or transmitted in any form by any means, electronic, mechanical, photocopying, recording or otherwise, without the prior written permission of the Publisher or a licence permitting restricted copying in the United Kingdom issued by the Copyright Licensing Agency Ltd, Barnard's Inn, 86 Fetter Lane, London, EC4A 1EN.

British Library Cataloguing-in-Publication Data
A catalogue record for this publication is available from the British Library.

Author: Anthea S. Thomas
Commissioning editor: Elaine Higgleton
Development editor: Bruce Nicholson
In-house editors: Caroline Green, Alexandra Wells, Holly Woolnough
Copy editor: Sue Chapple
Proof reader: Jan Schubert
Answer checker: Hugh Hillyard-Parker
Cover designers: Kevin Robbins and Gordon MacGilp
Cover image: Maquiladora/Shutterstock
Typesetter: QBS
Illustrators: QBS and Ann Paganuzzi
Production controller: Sarah Burke
Printed and Bound in the UK using 100% Renewable Electricity at CPI Group (UK) Ltd

This book is produced from independently certified FSC™ paper to ensure responsible forest management   .
For more information visit: www.harpercollins.co.uk/green

The publishers gratefully acknowledge the permission granted to reproduce the copyright material in this book. Every effort has been made to trace copyright holders and to obtain their permission for the use of copyright material. The publishers will gladly receive any information enabling them to rectify any error or omission at the first opportunity.

Answers available at www.collins.co.uk/Caribbean

Acknowledgements

The publishers wish to thank the following for permission to reproduce photographs. Every effort has been made to trace copyright holders and to obtain their permission for the use of copyright materials. The publishers will gladly receive any information enabling them to rectify any error or omission at the first opportunity.
(t = top, c = centre, b = bottom, l = left, r = right)

p41a Richard Whitcombe/Shutterstock; p41b Juneisy Q. Hawkins/Shutterstock; p41c Altin Osmanaj/Shutterstock; p41d Ramunas Bruzas/Shutterstock; p41e Delray Beach Photog/Shutterstock; p41f Janos Rautonen/Shutterstock; p41g PHB.cz (Richard Semik)/Shutterstock; p51tl Papakah/Shutterstock; p51tr Fasttailwind/Shutterstock; p51bl Dbimages/Alamy Stock Photo; p51br Pix/Alamy Stock Photo; p55 Bill Bachmann/Alamy Stock Photo; p56 Prometheus72/Shutterstock; p57 ARCTIC IMAGES/Alamy Stock Photo; p58 Xfilephotos/Shutterstock.

Contents

1 The Caribbean region

Student's Book pages 5–26

1 Circle the Caribbean region on this map of the world.

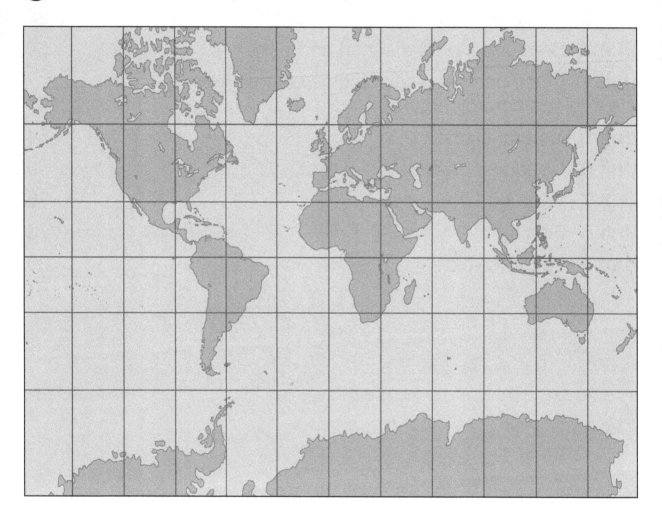

2 Read pages 5 and 6 in the Student's Book and describe where the Caribbean region is located.

_____

_____

_____

3 Read page 7 in the Student's Book and describe where Antigua and Barbuda is located in the Caribbean region.

_____

_____

_____

4 This map shows part of the Caribbean region. Colour the islands of Antigua and Barbuda.

5 On the map below, label the following countries and territories a–q:

a Anguilla

b Antigua and Barbuda

c Montserrat

d Dominica

e Saint Lucia

f Barbados

g St. Vincent and the Grenadines

h Grenada

i Cayman Islands

j St. Kitts and Nevis

k Cuba

l Dominican Republic

m Puerto Rico

n Jamaica

o Trinidad and Tobago

p Martinique

q British Virgin Islands

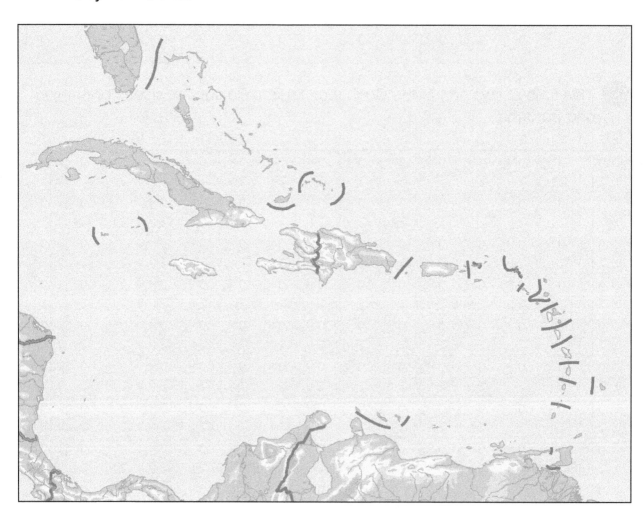

6 Write the name of each country shown. Then colour each one with a colour of your choice. Draw two more countries of your choice in the last two boxes and add the names of the countries.

Be careful! The maps are not drawn to the same scale.

a
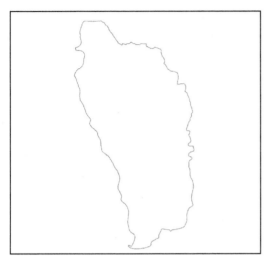

_____

b

_____

c

_____

d

_____

e

f

g

h

j

k

7 Write the name of each group of countries shown.

a

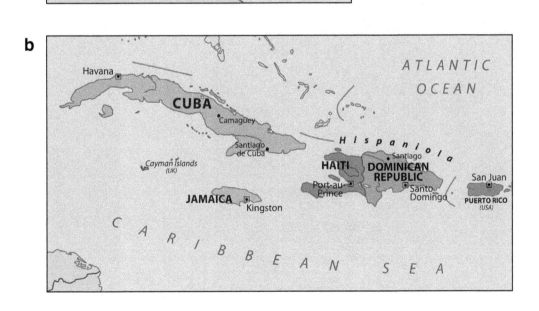

Virgin Is. (UK)
Anguilla (UK)
St-Martin (France)
Sint Maarten (Neth.)
St-Barthélemy (France)
Basseterre
Virgin Is. (USA)
ST KITTS AND NEVIS
ANTIGUA AND BARBUDA
St John's
Montserrat (UK)
Guadeloupe (France)
DOMINICA
Martinique (France)
ST LUCIA
ST VINCENT AND THE GRENADINES
BARBADOS
Bridgetown
GRENADA
St George's
Tobago
TRINIDAD AND TOBAGO
Port of Spain
Trinidad

_____

b

Havana
ATLANTIC OCEAN
CUBA
Camagüey
Santiago de Cuba
Hispaniola
Cayman Islands (UK)
Santiago
HAITI
DOMINICAN REPUBLIC
San Juan
Port-au-Prince
Santo Domingo
PUERTO RICO (USA)
JAMAICA
Kingston
CARIBBEAN SEA

_____

c

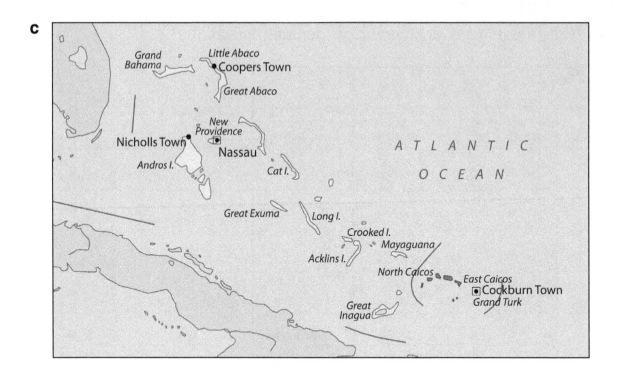

Grand Bahama

Little Abaco

●Coopers Town

Great Abaco

New Providence

Nicholls Town● ◉

Nassau

Andros I.

Cat I.

A T L A N T I C

O C E A N

Great Exuma

Long I.

Crooked I.

Mayaguana

Acklins I.

North Caicos

East Caicos

◉Cockburn Town

Grand Turk

Great Inagua

d

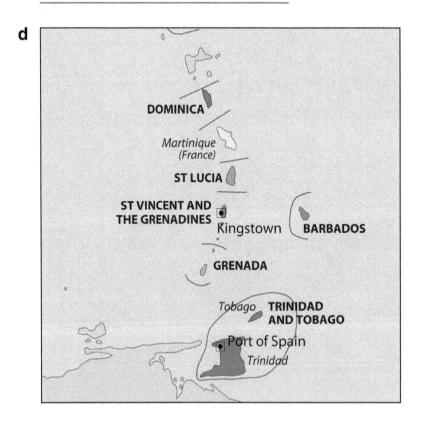

DOMINICA

Martinique (France)

ST LUCIA

ST VINCENT AND THE GRENADINES ◉

Kingstown

BARBADOS

GRENADA

Tobago

TRINIDAD AND TOBAGO

Port of Spain

Trinidad

e

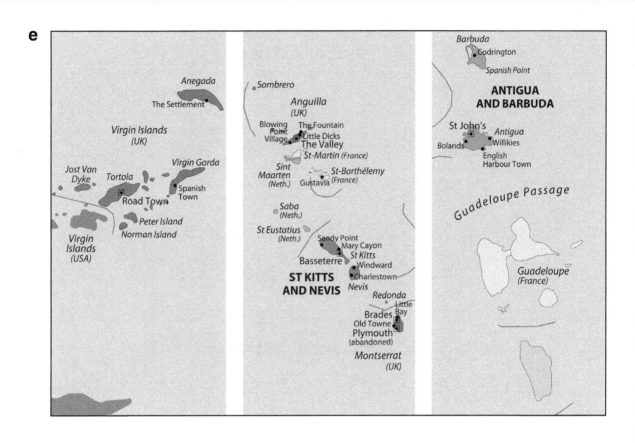

8 List the main islands which belong to each of the following island groups.

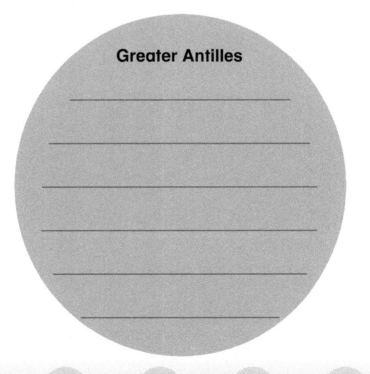

Greater Antilles

Lesser Antilles

_____ _____

_____ _____

_____ _____

_____ _____

_____ _____

Windward Islands

_____ _____

_____ _____

_____ _____

_____ _____

Leeward Islands

_____ _____

_____ _____

_____ _____

_____ _____

The ABC Islands

_____

_____

_____

The Virgin Islands

_____

_____

9 On this map of the Caribbean region, label all the bodies of water and continents that surround the region.

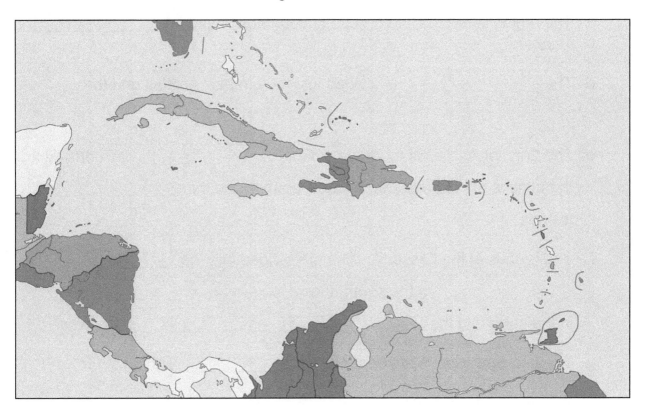

10 Read pages 5–16 in the Student's Book. Use words from the box to fill in the blank spaces in the sentences below.

> **Antilles**   **Caribbean region**   **Cayman**   **Central America**
>
> **Guadeloupe**   **geographical**   **Jamaica**   **Leeward Antilles**
>
> **Leeward Islands**   **Lesser Antilles**   **Leeward**
>
> **North America**   **Puerto Rico**   **South America**   **Windward Islands**

a   The _____ _____ consists of the Caribbean Sea, its islands and the surrounding coasts.

b   The region lies near the continents of _____ _____

and _____ _____, and near the region that is

called _____ _____.

c   The region is divided into groups of countries based on _____ location.

d   The _____ is divided into the Greater Antilles and the

_____ _____.

e   The Greater Antilles is made up of Cuba, _____, Puerto Rico,

the nations of Haiti and Dominican Republic and the _____

Islands.

f   The islands of the Lesser Antilles are divided into the _____

_____ in the south, the _____ _____

in the north and the _____ _____ in the west.

g   The Leeward Islands are east of _____, running southward

to _____.

h   The _____ Antilles are also known as the ABC islands.

11 Find the words related to the Caribbean region listed below in the wordsearch.

R	A	R	C	L	U	W	A	S	J	L	G	F	F	U
L	R	N	E	H	B	T	F	E	L	E	P	M	D	Q
G	B	W	T	S	E	V	Q	L	F	E	C	N	B	N
P	D	R	N	I	S	J	J	L	X	W	R	O	O	D
K	O	J	C	A	G	E	M	I	H	A	Y	R	R	W
N	A	M	I	K	E	U	L	T	Y	R	B	A	T	I
X	K	C	W	K	U	B	A	N	O	D	W	Q	S	S
G	R	E	A	T	E	R	B	A	D	D	U	L	F	H
T	I	E	E	B	W	F	F	I	N	A	A	N	A	U
Q	M	Q	K	W	U	T	U	I	R	N	L	O	Z	Y
S	P	U	O	R	G	Q	W	H	D	A	Q	I	J	E
J	S	T	M	E	Z	A	U	S	C	A	C	G	Q	X
S	O	U	T	H	K	P	T	D	W	W	E	E	L	O
G	Y	Q	U	I	Q	B	L	B	S	H	L	R	E	G
J	O	Z	P	A	J	G	W	I	P	L	Y	K	O	D

Antigua	Antilles	Caribbean	Greater
groups	islands	Leeward	Lesser
north	region	south	Windward

12 Complete the crossword. All the words are key vocabulary words from pages 8–17 in the Student's Book.

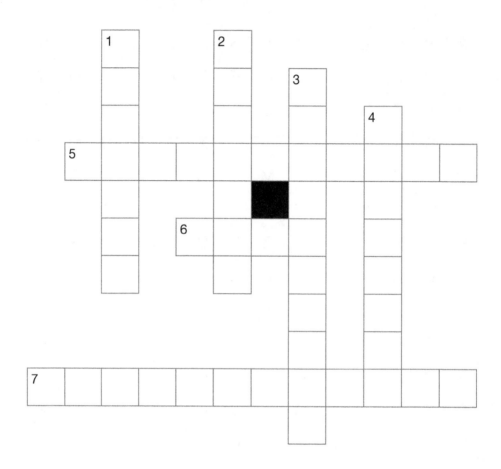

Across

5. An _____ is a series of islands. (11)

6. A country in the Greater Antilles (4)

7. Body of water that surrounds the islands in the Caribbean region (9, 3)

Down

1. The largest island in the US Virgin Islands (2, 5)

2. An island in the Lesser Antilles (7)

3. A chain of islands located to the north of the Greater Antilles (3, 7)

4. The most easterly Caribbean island (8)

13 Using the scale shown on the map, measure the distance of the lines shown.

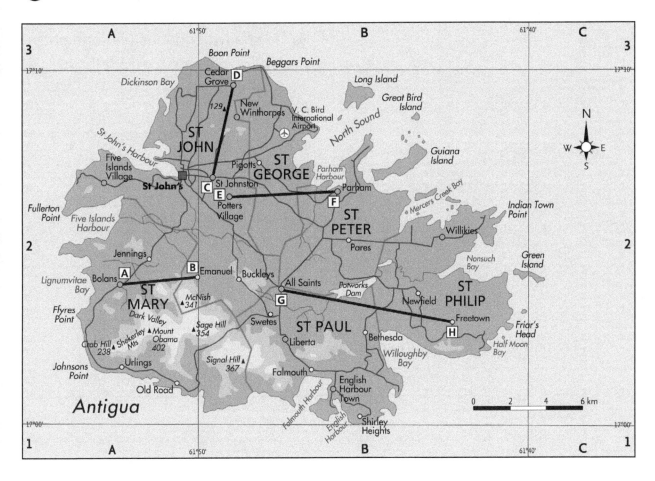

a Line AB _____

b Line CD _____

c Line EF _____

d Line GH _____

14 Use the map and key below, and the map on the previous page to find the following.

Features

National park
Point of interest
Major resort

Main airport
Port
Cruise ships
Major marina
Fishing port

St John's Cathedral
Museum of Antigua and Barbuda
Government House

Fort James
Fort
Barrington
St John's
Gunthorpes Sugar Factory
Sir Vivian Richards Cricket Stadium
Indian Town Point
Betty's Hope Sugar Estate
Devil's Bridge
Green Castle Hill
Harmony Hall
Jolly Harbour
Potworks Dam
Montpelier Sugar Factory
Mount Obama
Monk's Hill
Dow's Hill Interpretation Centre
Nelson's Dockyard
Shirley Heights

a Name two marinas and one port.

_____

_____

_____

_____

_____

_____

b Name three places of interest.

_____

_____

_____

_____

c Is Montpelier Sugar Factory a point of interest or a fishing port?

_____

d Which part of Antigua is the airport located in?

_____

e Where is Government House located?

_____

15 Use the map below to find the direction of:

a Swetes from All Saints

_____

b St. John's from Jennings

_____

c Pares to English Harbour Town

_____

d Shirley Heights to the airport

_____

e Newfield to Potters Village

_____

f Parham to Pigotts

_____

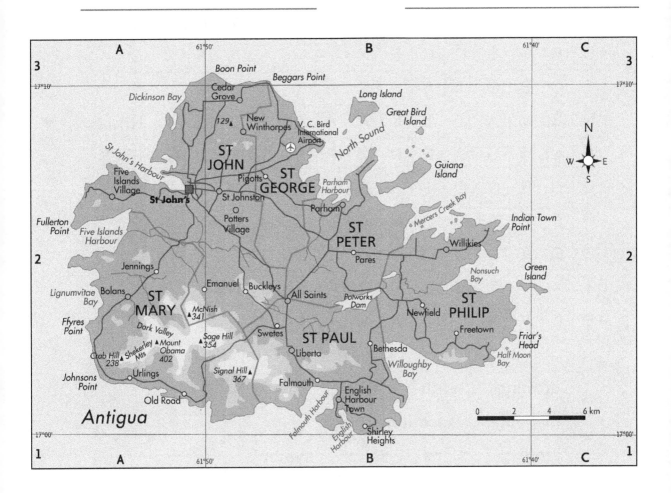

16 Find the words related to map-reading skills in the wordsearch. The words are all from pages 20–23 in the Student's Book.

A	H	M	L	P	S	S	H	O	W	S	T	H	E	L
O	C	T	A	T	I	O	L	N	O	F	I	M	P	O
R	T	A	R	N	T	O	F	O	E	A	T	U	R	E
S	O	N	T	A	C	H	E	E	B	A	R	T	H	S
S	U	R	F	A	E	A	C	G	E	M	B	A	L	B
Q	X	M	T	I	U	P	F	N	D	I	Y	H	Y	W
D	R	I	S	C	C	E	X	I	M	A	P	S	R	S
T	O	E	O	I	A	S	E	W	Z	B	S	S	L	S
N	B	M	A	T	G	K	A	A	F	T	J	L	T	H
E	L	W	U	D	E	N	X	R	O	S	I	D	T	B
U	R	R	G	O	I	J	S	D	Z	K	M	Q	B	H
O	E	G	A	U	G	N	A	L	S	M	S	E	T	T
S	O	Y	U	W	P	Q	G	I	N	G	D	R	F	G
I	X	I	S	V	B	H	Q	R	S	B	N	O	P	V
E	C	V	X	Y	I	A	Y	A	P	W	N	E	S	X

drawing   earth   features

language   location   map

reading   signs   skills   symbols

17 Read pages 24–25 in the Student's Book. Use words from the box to fill in the blank spaces in the sentences below.

Cancer   Capricorn   degrees (x2)   east

Equator   Greenwich Meridian   latitude

longitude   meridians   north

Prime Meridian   South   west (x2)

Lines of _____ run from east to _____

on a map or globe. They help us to locate places north or south of the

_____. They are measured in _____ north or

south. The main line of latitude is the Equator. Other lines of latitude include

the Tropics of _____ and _____, and the North

and _____ Pole.

Lines of _____ run from _____ to south on a

map or globe. They are also called _____. They are measured

in _____.

The most important line of longitude is called the _____

_____ (or the _____ _____).

These lines help us to locate places _____ or

_____ of the Prime Meridian.

18 Read pages 24–25 in the Student's Book. Look at this diagram of the Earth and label on it the following:

- The Equator

- The Tropic of Cancer

- The Tropic of Capricorn

- The Arctic Circle

- The North Pole

- The South Pole

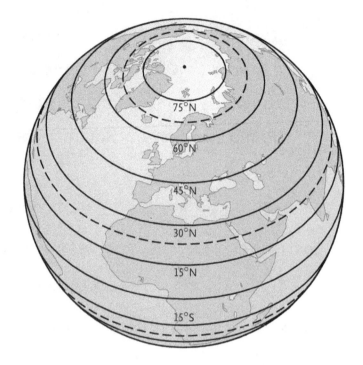

19 Read page 25 in the Student's Book. Use the words in the box to fill in the blanks in the sentences below.

> **coordinate**   **degree**   **latitude**
>
> **lines**   **location**   **weather**

A _____ is formed when a line of latitude meets a line of

longitude. They give us the exact _____ of places. They are

useful for _____ forecasters, ship captains and pilots.

A coordinate is written using the _____ for the

_____ of latitude and longitude. The line of

_____ is always written first when writing a coordinate.

20 Use coordinates to give the location of the following places. Give your answer to the nearest whole degree.

Port-au-Prince _____

San Juan _____

Barbuda _____

Saint Lucia _____

Curacao _____

Havana _____

Grenada _____

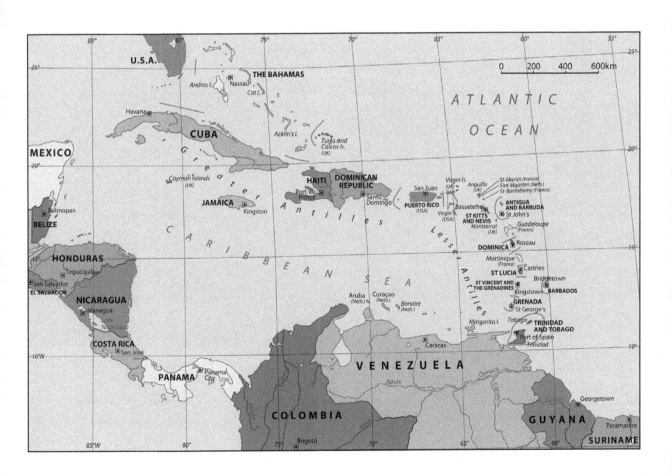

2 Parishes in Antigua and Barbuda

Student's Book pages 27–38

1 Unscramble the names of the parishes of Antigua.

a St lupa _____

b St rptee _____

c St ryma _____

d tS jnho _____

e St eoregg _____

f tS ilhppi _____

2 Read page 27 of the Student's Book and add the names of the parishes to this map.

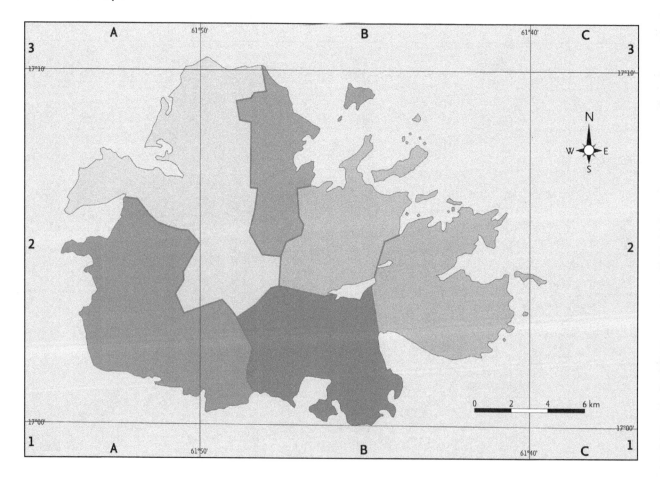

3 Complete the table with the correct information about the parishes in Antigua.

Name of parish	Capital	Size of parish	Population
St. John			
St. Mary			
St. Peter			
St. Philip			
St. Paul			
St. George			

4 Read page 27 in the Student's Book. Use words from the box to fill in the blanks in the sentences below.

> Anglican   capital   coast   divided   fire station   load
>
> parks   police station   ports   six   St. George   St. John
>
> St. Mary   St. Paul   St. Peter   St. Phillip   unload   utility

a   The island of Antigua is _____ into _____ parishes.

b   The parishes in Antigua are _____, _____,

   _____, _____, _____ and

   _____.

c   The main town of each parish is called the _____.

d   Parish capitals are usually provided with _____ services

   such as electricity and water, and facilities such as a _____

   _____ and _____.

e   Each parish capital has a parish church which is usually an

   _____ Church.

f   Some parish capitals are located on the _____, while some
   are inland.

g   Some parish capitals have _____. This is where ships come

   to _____ and _____.

5 Read pages 28–34 in the Student's Book. Match each feature to its parish.

a pottery

b Mount Obama

c Betty's Hope

d Pineapple Beach

e Nelson's Dockyard

f Deep Water Harbour

i St. John

ii St. Paul

iii St. Mary

iv St. George

v St. Peter

vi St. Phillip

6 Read pages 35–38 in the Student's Book. Then read the statements below and circle True or False for each one.

a There are five different types of soil found in Antigua.   True   False

b Volcanic soil can be found on the southern side of the island. True   False

c Volcanic soil is not good for growing plants.   True   False

d Limestone is used in making cement.   True   False

e Clay soil is found on the eastern side of the island.   True   False

f Clay soil is good for making pottery.   True   False

g Barbuda has a mixture of clay and limestone soil.   True   False

h Sea View Farm is one village that clay soil can be found in.   True   False

i Limestone can be added to soil to make it fertile.   True   False

7 Find words related to parishes in Antigua and Barbuda in the wordsearch.

J	Y	W	S	J	D	Y	Y	B	Y	R	B	V	L	T
Y	Y	N	Q	V	Q	R	P	H	N	U	D	I	Q	O
K	F	I	E	Y	E	R	W	X	I	D	O	Q	Y	H
S	E	R	U	T	A	E	F	L	L	S	P	L	P	T
S	Z	I	T	O	S	X	D	N	L	S	Y	A	B	P
Z	E	O	N	S	T	I	C	L	I	V	F	T	E	A
O	P	G	C	V	N	P	J	A	A	A	S	I	C	G
Z	W	U	A	G	E	S	H	U	T	T	M	P	H	P
F	S	D	E	L	Q	C	P	D	M	A	S	A	U	D
K	H	Y	Z	V	L	K	O	A	D	C	J	C	R	N
N	H	O	J	T	S	I	R	R	R	H	R	W	C	W
V	C	W	A	P	K	Y	V	G	B	I	Z	W	H	O
A	N	T	I	G	U	A	J	P	D	L	S	M	R	T
N	N	X	R	Z	A	F	X	J	V	X	S	H	K	O
L	Y	L	O	G	I	A	Z	E	N	S	I	Z	E	B

> **Antigua**   **building**   **capital**
> **church**   **features**   **main**   **parish**
> **pottery**   **size**   **soil**   **St John**
> **St Mary**   **town**   **villages**

8 Complete the crossword puzzle. The clues are about the parishes of Antigua.

Across

2 The airport can be found in this parish.

4 Parham can be found in this parish.

5 Nelson's Dockyard can be found here.

Down

1 The capital of Antigua

2 The village of Bolans can be found here.

3 This parish is located on the most easterly part of the island.

3 Settlement patterns then and now

Student's Book pages 39–50

1 Read pages 42–43 in the Student's Book. Use words from the box to fill in the blanks in the text below.

Arawaks	baskets	cacique	cassava
clay	cone-shaped	cotton fibres	feathers
gods	hammocks	hunting	laws	mud
pepper-pot	potatoes	pottery	shells
spears	spirits	strong	thatched

The first group of people to settle in the Antigua were the

_____.

They were gentle people who shared their possessions and food with

each other. The Arawak leader was called a _____.

He made all the _____ and lived in the best

house in the village. His clothes were beautiful, decorated with

_____ and _____. He had to be

wise and _____ to control his people.

The Arawaks lived in _____ houses with

_____ roofs. The walls were made with reeds and

_____. There were _____ and

_____ pots inside the houses, but no furniture.

They grew fruit and vegetables to eat. The women used sticks

to dig holes and planted _____ and sweet

_____. They made cassareep from the cassava juice.

They used the cassareep to make _____.

The men went _____ and fishing. They used wooden

_____, fish traps and nets to catch the fish.

They made a lot of things from the natural resources around them.

They made _____ with red clay, hammocks from

_____ and _____ from grass. They

worshipped _____ that lived in the world around them.

They also worshipped the _____ of their ancestors.

2 Read pages 43–44 in the Student's Book. Use words from the box to fill in the blanks in the text below.

> **Caribs**   **cassava**   **evil**   **fished**   **good**
>
> **healed**   **huts**   **iguana**   **Lesser Antilles**
>
> **Ouboutu**   **pepper**   **priest**   **rectangular**
>
> **sickness**   **tobacco**   **warlike**   **warrior**   **yams**

The _____ settled mainly in the _____ on

islands like Grenada, St. Vincent and the Grenadines, and Dominica, as well

as in the north and west of Trinidad.

The Caribs were more _____ than the Arawaks. Their

leader was called the _____. He had to be a strong

_____ and he made the laws for the people. The

_____ was also very important. He _____

people who were ill with bush medicines.

The Caribs built large _____ houses for the men and the

older boys. The boys were trained to be warriors and priests. The women

and children lived in small _____. In the houses there were

hammocks, a few clay pots and wooden stools.

The women grew _____, _____,

sweet potatoes and _____. The men hunted and

_____. The Carib's favourite food was cassava cooked

with crab and _____. They also liked eating the flesh of the

_____.

The Caribs believed that there are _____ and

_____ spirits. The bad spirits caused _____

and death.

3 Read pages 42–44 in the Student's Book. Fill in the table to show the similarities and differences between the Caribs and Arawaks.

Similarities	Differences

4 Read pages 44–45 in the Student's Book. Use words from the box to fill in the blanks in the text below.

> Arawaks   British   buy   cattle
>
> diseases   Dutch   Europe   Europeans
>
> French   gold   pigs   Spanish
>
> sugar   survived   tobacco

After the Amerindians came the _____. They came

from the continent of _____. The _____

were first and they were looking for _____ and silver.

Next came the _____, the _____ and

the _____. Some wanted to plant sugarcane and

_____ while others wanted to _____ and

sell things.

The Spanish made the _____ slaves and forced them to

work very hard. Many died from the hard work and the _____

brought by the Europeans. The Caribs were warlike, and they fought the

Spanish, but only a few _____.

The Europeans brought important crops such as _____, and

animals like goats, _____ and _____.

5 Use words from the box to fill in the blanks in the text below.

> badly   beaten   dialect   Europeans
>
> forced   slaves   sugar   traditions
>
> West Africans

The _____ came to Antigua and the Caribbean from the

continent of Africa. They were brought here by the _____.

After the Amerindians died, they had no one to work for them so they went

to Africa and _____ the Africans to come. They were called

_____.

They worked on the _____ plantations and were treated very

_____ by the Europeans. They were _____

and sold to the highest bidder.

Many of the _____ that we have today were started by the

Africans. These include our _____, our dance and our music.

6 Find words related to settlements in the wordsearch.

N	T	S	H	S	E	I	N	D	D	A	I	A	N	S
A	A	N	K	D	B	C	H	I	I	B	N	E	S	E
C	A	C	M	A	E	I	S	T	O	O	T	H	E	C
A	R	I	I	B	W	C	R	A	B	L	E	A	N	T
O	W	O	R	R	O	A	U	A	K	I	A	S	I	N
D	U	N	T	V	F	G	R	E	C	S	R	E	E	D
L	A	B	E	C	I	A	O	A	U	H	R	U	E	R
S	A	R	F	T	A	T	T	E	R	E	S	R	L	A
V	E	E	N	R	Y	R	W	S	I	D	F	O	A	S
D	A	A	B	O	L	I	I	N	E	S	O	P	H	E
Y	R	E	V	A	L	S	D	B	D	W	O	E	A	D
U	R	E	S	E	N	I	H	C	B	J	D	A	Q	C
I	R	W	C	S	A	Y	B	U	A	E	V	N	F	Y
X	Q	Q	P	N	M	J	F	T	M	F	A	S	N	R
R	D	Q	S	S	O	U	T	G	M	R	O	N	C	Q

abolished	Antigua	Arawaks
Caribbean	Caribs	Chinese
discovered	Europeans	food
Indians	slavery	West African

7 Draw a line from each word on the left to its definition on the right.

a settlement

b emancipation

c culture

d Amerindians

e traditions

f slave

g ethnic group

h indigenous

i Originally present in a place

ii The first people of the Caribbean

iii A person who is the legal property of another person and is forced to obey them

iv The customs, arts, shared language, history and ideas of a group

v A group of people who identify with each other based on common language, ancestry or culture

vi Beliefs, behaviours and actions that people hand down from one generation to the next

vii Being set free from control by other people

viii A place where people establish a community

8 Unscramble the words relating to groups of people who settled in the Caribbean.

a HEICNES _____

b ADINSIN _____

c MINAASENDIR _____

d OENSUEAPR _____

e SNFCRIAA _____

f SSNIRYA _____

9 Arrange the words in question 8 in the order in which they came to the Caribbean.

_____

_____

_____

_____

_____

10 Match each ethnic group with the reason why they came to the Caribbean.

a Africans

b Indians and Chinese

c Amerinidians

d Europeans

i To settle and look for food

ii To work as slaves

iii To look for gold and silver

iv To work on plantations with a contract

11 Each ethnic group that came to the Caribbean brought their own culture with them. Fill in the table to show aspects of our culture today that comes from the different ethnic groups.

Ethnic group	Aspects of our culture
Amerindian	
Europeans	
Indian	
Chinese	
Africans	
North Americans	

12 Find words related to settlements in the wordsearch.

E	R	I	Y	T	D	D	X	S	X	S	Q	Z	B	D
O	Y	R	J	R	R	I	W	K	N	B	E	F	E	P
J	D	C	P	A	E	B	S	A	O	U	A	L	S	M
D	X	M	H	D	F	T	I	C	R	W	T	Z	L	V
X	L	N	K	I	V	D	T	O	O	T	D	K	D	V
Y	S	D	I	T	N	G	P	O	E	V	T	O	R	M
J	X	F	H	I	D	E	Q	S	P	M	E	N	Q	W
U	V	G	R	O	A	P	S	Y	I	Y	R	R	A	I
O	M	E	I	N	D	I	G	E	N	O	U	S	E	A
A	M	R	S	K	C	O	M	M	A	H	T	Q	T	D
A	A	I	N	D	I	A	N	S	N	X	L	E	H	E
H	F	J	M	A	J	J	P	Q	Y	N	U	M	N	Z
B	B	P	O	T	Y	E	M	G	Y	V	C	U	I	Y
F	G	Z	Y	S	P	T	S	H	K	A	D	R	C	N
D	Q	Y	T	M	P	E	Z	G	E	H	N	I	D	E

Amerindians   Chinese   culture

discovered   ethnic   Europeans

hammocks   Indians   indigenous

pottery   settled   tradition

40

4 The Caribbean: sustainable environment and natural features

Student's Book pages 51–72

1 Write the name of each of these natural features found in the Caribbean.

a

_____

e

_____

b

_____

f

_____

c

_____

d

_____

g

_____

2 Find words related to natural features in Antigua in the wordsearch.

Y	T	V	Q	L	A	I	K	N	Q	Y	F	I	X	E	R	M	B	P	I
S	R	U	I	E	F	R	Y	A	C	B	W	W	S	Y	F	A	A	G	U
N	I	A	T	N	U	O	M	H	S	I	N	C	M	G	X	D	T	R	A
Y	S	T	U	M	Z	N	H	N	D	I	C	A	P	C	N	S	C	P	I
V	B	I	L	T	N	J	W	S	F	K	D	H	K	H	G	K	A	B	L
W	P	R	G	F	C	E	C	V	O	S	B	E	Q	R	E	R	V	K	S
Q	R	T	S	N	T	N	A	N	G	F	F	D	E	I	W	O	E	M	U
I	O	R	G	L	A	X	A	N	P	B	Z	E	N	S	J	W	S	D	Z
I	B	E	A	S	V	L	I	S	V	K	N	X	W	T	B	T	C	A	G
Z	D	N	R	B	K	L	H	R	D	C	U	S	S	I	C	O	N	S	F
F	D	U	N	M	L	S	T	I	A	R	L	G	W	A	Z	P	D	N	M
S	G	B	O	A	D	G	L	S	L	Q	I	O	A	N	O	O	G	A	L
E	T	M	W	V	I	O	T	I	N	L	Q	B	T	V	T	S	H	M	S
L	C	E	P	F	T	L	M	O	U	N	T	O	B	A	M	A	N	V	Z
L	U	F	O	S	E	G	K	K	J	C	O	G	C	L	G	I	N	U	U
A	P	M	M	H	C	I	K	I	W	G	I	W	K	L	I	E	H	U	S
S	W	O	I	C	V	Y	J	U	R	U	Z	U	J	E	W	M	E	T	L
T	S	L	N	H	A	U	O	P	C	P	J	O	G	Y	L	E	M	X	L
R	L	W	G	H	R	F	E	Q	M	N	N	H	U	M	N	V	Q	N	N
R	B	T	U	C	F	E	Z	P	R	D	J	R	C	I	Q	N	V	P	V

bat cave	**bird sanctuary**	**Christian Valley**
Green Castle Hill	**lagoon**	**McNish Mountain**
Mount Obama	**Potworks Dam**	**Signal Hill**
Wallings Dam	**wetlands**	

3 On the map of Antigua, write in the names of the following natural features where they are located. Use the map on page 23 of the Student's book to help.

Long Island   Willoughby Bay   Mount Obama

Potworks Dam   Signal Hill   Indian Town Point

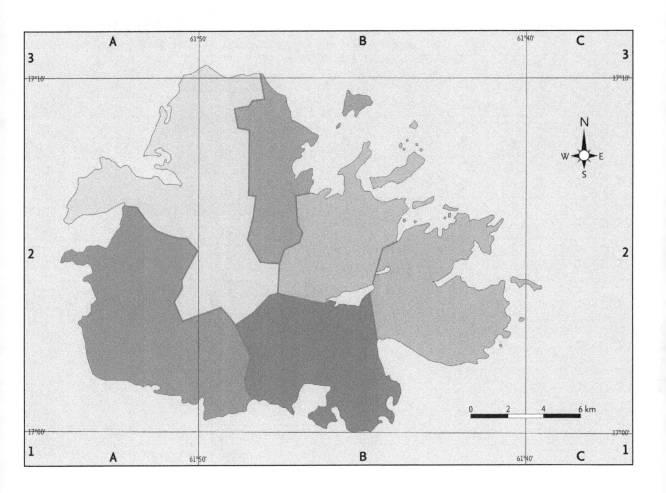

4 On the map of Barbuda, write in the names of the following natural features. Use the map on page 23 of the Student's book to help.

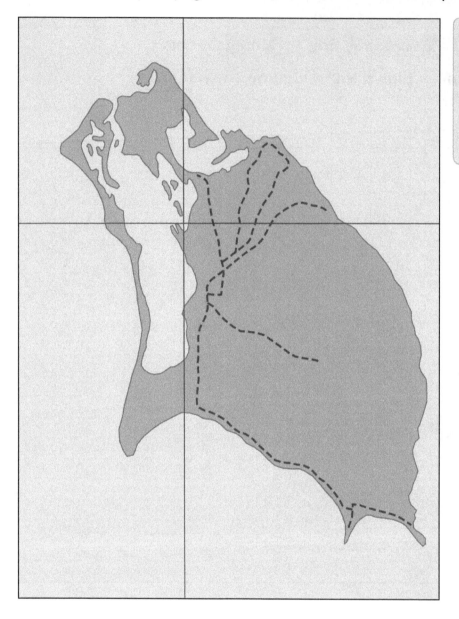

Codrington Lagoon

Palmetto Point

Cobb Cove

The Highlands

5 Read pages 54–59 in the Student's Book. Fill in the table below to give an example of each natural feature. Say which island each one is in.

Natural feature	Name	Country
Beach		
Hill		
Mangrove		
Rainforest		
River		
Swamp		
Cave		
Volcano		
Hot springs		
Waterfall		

6 Draw a circle around all the things that make up the natural environment in Antigua and Barbuda.

soil   garden   animals

schools   churches   trees

beaches   roads   hills   dams

air   weather   rubbish dumps

7 Read pages 60–62 in the Student's Book. Complete the spider diagram to show some of the main factors responsible for the changes to our natural environment.

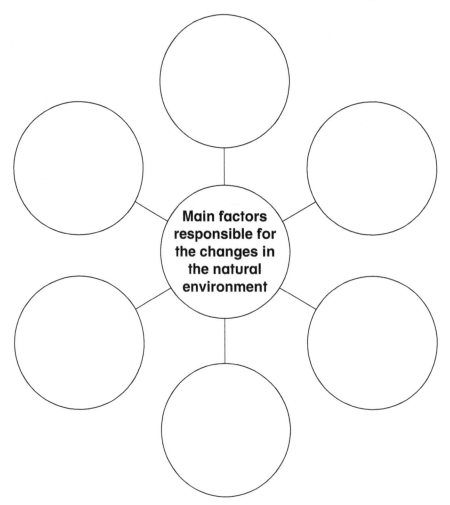

Main factors responsible for the changes in the natural environment

8 Read pages 62–63 in the Student's Book. Match each word in the column on the left with its correct definition on the right.

a deforestation

b reclamation

c excavation

d farming

e building

f afforestation

i The conversion of unsuitable land into land suitable for building or farming

ii Growing plants and/or rearing animals

iii The planting of trees to replace ones that have been cut down

iv The process of constructing something

v Digging into the earth

vi The clearing of a forest of trees so that the land can be used for something else

9 Read pages 62–68 in the Student's Book. What are some of ways in which the natural environment may be misused in Antigua and Barbuda?

_____

_____

_____

_____

_____

_____

10 Explain, in your own words, what is meant by conservation.

_____

_____

_____

11 State three conservation laws that are used to protect the natural environment in Antigua and Barbuda.

_____

_____

_____

12 Write one law (your own choice) that you would like the government to use in helping to protect the natural environment.

_____

_____

_____

_____

13 Look at these signs. Circle the signs that you think are concerned with conservation.

Conservation Area
Ground nesting birds

PLEASE
TURN OUT
LIGHTS WHEN
NOT IN USE

Please **DO NOT DISTURB** *Thank You*

NO
PARKING

DO NOT
LITTER

HOME
FOR SALE

THINK GREEN
CONSERVE
WATER

14 Find words related to pollution in the wordsearch.

K	S	O	N	V	A	E	S	N	M	S	N	G	G	Q
X	U	L	I	O	H	T	S	D	N	R	O	H	G	Q
S	S	L	A	T	F	I	W	A	K	E	I	M	W	J
P	A	R	E	M	C	Y	M	R	E	X	S	K	G	Q
Z	I	C	W	K	I	U	Y	V	H	I	E	Y	D	B
W	R	C	N	S	H	N	F	U	M	E	S	I	R	Q
V	A	E	V	Q	P	L	A	S	O	S	R	A	E	V
Q	S	T	C	C	O	F	B	P	O	T	E	L	T	W
S	W	J	E	S	L	S	S	U	Y	S	A	X	T	B
D	L	M	S	R	L	E	G	A	B	R	A	G	I	D
N	U	R	O	A	U	H	T	A	E	D	D	B	L	N
J	A	S	P	V	T	C	H	V	C	F	I	R	E	A
C	I	E	T	O	I	I	E	T	S	P	P	D	Q	L
S	D	L	L	I	O	I	J	E	P	Q	I	Y	J	Y
V	M	X	I	C	N	V	A	E	H	F	P	A	G	S

air   animals   cars   clean   death

dirty   dust   fire   fumes   garbage

humans   land   litter   noise   oil

pollution   sea   sickness   water

15 Read pages 64–68 in the Student's Book. Use words from the box to fill in the blanks in the text below.

air	**dirty**	**four**	**fumes**	**land**	**littering**
noise	**planes**	**pollution**	**sewage**	**water**	

When we make the environment around us _____, harmful

or uncomfortable for us, it is called _____. There are

_____ main types of pollution.

_____ pollution is making the land around us dirty by

_____, for example by throwing or dumping our garbage in

areas that are not intended for it.

_____ pollution is the introduction of garbage,

_____, oil and other items, that may cause harm to the

creatures that live in the water.

_____ pollution comes from human activities releasing gases

into the air. These cause damage to living things and the environment, for

example toxic _____ from burning garbage, factories, and car

exhaust fumes.

_____ pollution comes from sounds that can cause damage to

the human ear. It can be caused by _____ and cars, as well

as by recreational activities such as jet skiing.

16 Look at the pictures and say what type of pollution each one is showing.

a

_____

b

_____

c

_____

d

_____

17 For each type of pollution in the table, write some of the effects it can have on humans and the environment.

Type of pollution	Effects on humans	Effects on the environment
Land		
Water		
Air		
Noise		

18 Explain some of the ways in which pollution can be reduced in Antigua and Barbuda.

_____

_____

_____

_____

19 Complete the diagram to show some of the causes and the consequences of each of these environmental problems.

Causes

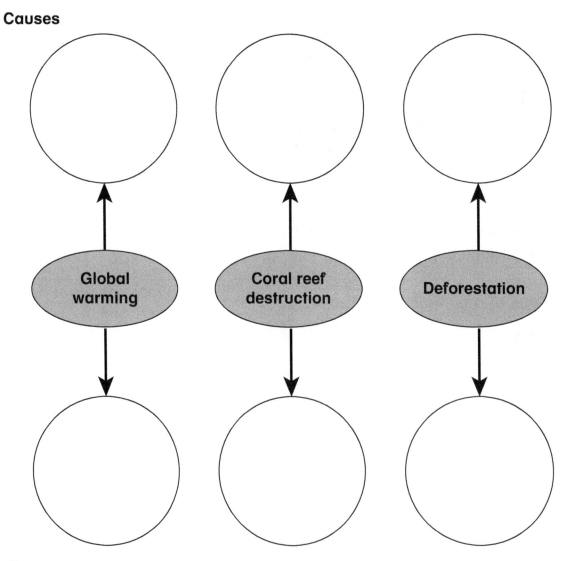

Consequences

20 Read pages 68–72 in the Student's Book. Make a note of some of the things we can do to help the following.

a Reduce the emission of greenhouse gases

_____

_____

_____

_____

_____

b Stop or reduce coral reef destruction

_____

_____

_____

_____

_____

c Reduce deforestation.

_____

_____

_____

_____

_____

5 Natural disasters

Student's Book pages 73–91

1 Find words related to natural disasters in the wordsearch.

T	J	X	R	R	S	S	O	F	W	U	S	A	L	V
N	S	B	X	P	E	N	D	I	A	S	O	U	A	T
P	Q	U	I	N	A	T	N	E	E	W	R	R	N	H
M	D	R	N	C	O	D	A	N	M	O	D	M	D	G
A	A	H	L	A	S	I	D	W	O	O	G	R	S	U
L	W	O	U	P	M	E	T	E	F	V	Q	M	L	O
K	V	U	E	R	R	I	D	P	Y	O	E	Z	I	R
O	J	E	E	A	R	T	H	Q	U	A	K	E	D	D
D	D	B	P	Z	P	I	D	B	Z	R	V	B	E	X
X	U	E	A	O	X	C	R	A	G	E	H	C	M
N	R	D	O	O	L	F	D	A	S	D	I	A	U	W
P	W	W	S	U	O	R	E	G	N	A	D	Z	Z	W
H	U	Y	A	X	V	L	T	D	A	E	O	A	T	N
D	O	R	M	A	N	T	Z	J	L	G	R	R	D	X
R	E	P	V	K	Y	N	Q	O	D	O	F	D	A	E

dangerous	**dormant**	**drought**	**earthquake**
eruption	**flood**	**hazard**	**hurricane**
landslide	**preparedness**	**spiral**	**tsunami**
volcano	**water**	**windspeed**	

2 Use a phrase from the box to fill in the blank space in each sentence below.

> **natural disaster**   **natural event**   **natural hazard**

a A _____ _____ occurs outside of human control.

b A _____ _____ is the threat of a natural event that will have a negative effect on people or the environment.

c A _____ _____ can be the consequence of a natural hazard.

3 Write a list of as many types of natural disaster as you can.

_____

_____

_____

_____

4 Look at this picture taken after a hurricane and then answer the questions that follow.

a Briefly explain the causes of this type of disaster.

_____

_____

b List two things that can be done to lessen the effects of this type of disaster.

Before it happens:

_____

_____

During the time it is happening:

_____

_____

After the disaster:

_____

_____

c How can this disaster cause the environment to change?

_____

_____

5 Look at this picture taken after an earthquake and then answer the questions that follow.

a Briefly explain the causes of this type of disaster.

_____

_____

b List some of the damage that this disaster can cause to the environment and to humans.

_____

_____

_____

c Use the internet to research this question. What is one suggestion that you can make to the people living in this area that would lessen the damage in the event of another disaster like this one?

_____

_____

_____

6 Look at this picture taken during a volcanic eruption and then answer the questions that follow.

a Briefly explain the causes of this type of disaster.

_____

_____

b Name one Caribbean island that can be affected by a disaster like this.

_____

_____

c What damage can this disaster do to the environment?

_____

_____

d How can it be helpful to the environment?

_____

_____

7 Look at the picture and answer the questions that follow.

a What natural disaster is shown in the picture?

_____

b Explain briefly why this event happens.

_____

_____

c Explain the effect this event can have on the environment.

_____

_____

_____

8 Briefly explain how each of these organisations work to help us in times of natural disasters.

a NODS

_____

_____

b Red Cross

_____

_____

c CDEMA

_____

_____

6 Cottage industries

Student's Book pages 92–96

1 Read pages 92–95 in the Student's Book. Use words from the box to fill in the blanks in the sentences below.

> beneficial   cottage   employees   family
>
> food   quality   skin products   small

a A _____ industry is a business activity that is done in a home.

This is a local business operated in a home with few _____,

mainly the _____ members.

b _____ and _____ are examples of products that

may be produced in a cottage industry.

c In Antigua, cottage industries are _____ in size compared to

other large-scale industries in operation.

d When people shop from a local cottage industry they can be sure that the

products they are getting are fresh and are of a good _____.

e Operating a cottage industry is very _____ to the people in

the country.

2 Match each type of cottage industry on the left with a possible product on the right.

a food			**i** steel pan	
b clothing			**ii** shoes	
c jewelry			**iii** dress	
d art and craft			**iv** hair products	
e personal care			**v** beaded necklaces	
f leather			**vi** hot sauce	

3 Put these tiles into the correct order to reveal a message. Write the results in the blank tiles below. Three have been done for you.

A G E	S U A L	O M E	A H	E S U	S T R I
E I N	N V O L	R I N G	I N D U	C O T T	L Y I
V E M	D O N	A C T U	A N U F		

		I N D U			S U A L
		V E M			

60

4 Use the internet to research this question. For each of the locally-made products listed below, write the names of the raw materials used to make the product.

Product	Raw material
Sugarcake	
Raspberry jam	
Hot sauce	
Cake	
Ice cream	
Soap	

5 Read page 95 of the Student's Book. Briefly explain some of the benefits cottage industries bring to Antigua and Barbuda.

_____

_____

_____

_____

_____

_____

_____

_____

_____

6 Use the internet to research this question. Briefly outline the steps that need to be taken to produce a locally-made product of your choice from start to finish.

_____

_____

_____

_____

_____

_____

_____

_____

_____

7 Unscramble each of the clue words. Copy the letters in the numbered cells to other cells with the same number on the next page.

GOECATT

43	65				7	

DINRUYTS

21	31	10	62	36	13	19

RANUNTUFMICGA

80		82	11	37			60		28	32	53

LSLAM

12	55		56	

SESBIUSN

	63	15		35	42	45

LCLYOLA

24	1			58	

DOPRUCTS

18	39	38	22		4	73

PUENERTESNERR

67		29	50	59	25	69	23	9	54	52	41

WAR EATSRIMLA

	46			5		76	78	34	77	72	70

LOICHNGT

71	27	33	47	68		6

WYJLERE

64		40		14	

JASM

	17		

SOPSA

2	49	26		

TONCOUC LOI

75		61	44	30	74		48	8	

NEHOY

66	57	79	16	83

TYLEOHOCGN

3	51			20		81		

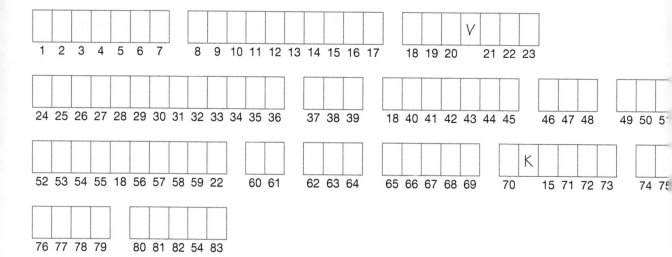

1 2 3 4 5 6 7   8 9 10 11 12 13 14 15 16 17   18 19 20 V 21 22 23

24 25 26 27 28 29 30 31 32 33 34 35 36   37 38 39   18 40 41 42 43 44 45   46 47 48   49 50 51

52 53 54 55 18 56 57 58 59 22   60 61   62 63 64   65 66 67 68 69   70 K 15 71 72 73   74 75

76 77 78 79   80 81 82 54 83

8 Find words related to cottage industries in the wordsearch.

F	T	M	D	U	L	L	T	D	E	I	Y	G	P	L
A	A	E	D	J	A	H	S	N	N	J	N	S	A	G
M	Q	H	C	B	E	E	W	D	I	I	A	A	C	V
I	X	U	E	H	I	C	U	H	R	R	I	X	K	Z
L	G	L	A	L	N	S	U	U	Y	X	P	E	A	E
Y	S	N	L	L	T	O	T	A	D	F	D	M	G	G
R	Q	E	U	R	I	C	L	P	S	O	R	O	I	A
L	J	D	Y	M	A	T	P	O	O	T	N	H	N	T
J	A	M	S	F	S	F	Y	F	G	Z	O	R	G	T
R	P	L	U	R	T	H	T	S	W	Y	S	H	N	O
Q	P	N	C	U	V	L	E	A	T	H	E	R	F	C
W	A	D	D	P	D	Z	W	Z	Q	Z	N	E	S	Y
M	I	N	T	E	R	N	A	T	I	O	N	A	L	I
E	E	Y	O	L	P	M	E	H	S	E	R	F	V	R
S	I	H	K	N	I	E	C	M	R	Z	M	G	S	W

cottage   employee   family   food

fresh   home   hot sauce   industry

international   jams   jellies   labels

leather   manufacturing   packaging

print   quality   technology

7 Work and occupation

Student's Book pages 97–105

1 Read pages 97–100 in the Student's Book and answer these questions.

a In your own words, explain the meaning of the word 'work'.

_____

_____

_____

b In your own words, explain the meaning of the word 'occupation'.

_____

_____

_____

c What are the two ways in which a person can be employed in Antigua and Barbuda?

_____

_____

_____

d Give all the reasons you can think of why people work.

_____

_____

_____

2 When a person works, what benefits does it bring to:

a an individual?

_____

_____

b the family?

_____

_____

c the community?

_____

_____

3 Complete the following table. Give as many reasons as you can.

Reasons why people work	Reasons why people do not work

4 Find words related to work and occupations in the wordsearch.

B	S	B	S	V	E	H	U	R	F	U	F	B	Q	Q
N	C	G	T	A	F	G	E	Q	H	N	S	I	K	M
W	F	E	N	V	L	Y	E	W	I	E	W	L	S	T
E	G	A	W	I	O	A	O	D	L	M	W	L	R	G
X	F	E	N	L	N	R	R	F	Y	P	P	S	O	Y
I	V	E	P	R	K	R	E	Y	O	L	A	Y	J	U
T	Y	M	B	Z	T	M	A	L	G	O	Q	J	E	B
I	E	P	X	H	P	H	C	E	Q	Y	S	B	E	N
Z	N	W	Y	L	N	T	V	L	C	M	B	B	Y	F
O	F	P	O	D	H	S	T	U	D	E	N	T	O	Y
Z	L	Y	F	N	J	D	Z	C	E	N	L	Y	L	J
T	E	U	X	X	B	N	C	L	K	T	Y	X	P	E
D	Y	I	Z	M	R	M	L	H	U	U	W	I	M	D
K	I	N	N	O	I	T	A	P	U	C	C	O	E	F
S	B	L	C	G	C	M	V	R	D	U	B	Y	V	R

bills   earnings   employee   employer

jobs   occupation   salary   self-employed

unemployment   wage   work

5 Circle all the ways that you think people can use to try and find a job.

Looking at signs   Staying at home

Visiting a business to ask about jobs

Word of mouth   Liming on the block   Searching newspapers

Searching the internet   Sleeping all day

6 Read pages 101–103 in the Student's Book. In your own words, explain about the three main types of worker. Give some examples of each type.

_____

_____

_____

_____

_____

_____

_____

_____

_____

7 Use a word from the box to fill in the blank at the start of each statement about unemployment below.

> **Technical**   **Cyclical**   **Structural**   **Seasonal**

a _____ unemployment occurs when the demand for particular goods and services in some industries has dropped off, such as in the tourist inductry when there are no tourists in the hotels.

b _____ unemployment is caused by machines replacing human labour.

c _____ unemployment happens when there is a change in demand from one product or service to another, which may call for different skills. The workers that do not have the skills necessary for the new product or service lose their jobs.

d _____unemployment is when the general economy is weak. Industries may cut back and lay off workers.

8 Match each word on the left with its correct definition on the right.

a employee

b occupation

c wage

d work

e unemployed

f employer

g salary

h self-employed

i An activity involving effort done in order to achieve a result

ii A fixed regular payment earned for work or services paid on a daily or weekly basis

iii A fixed regular payment, usually paid on a monthly basis

iv A person or organisation that employs people

v A person employed for wages or salary

vi A person who works for him or herself

vii A person without a paid job but available to work

viii A job or profession

9 Give some of the reasons why you think a person may be unemployed.

_____

_____

_____

_____

_____

_____

_____

10 If the main earner in a family becomes unemployed, how might that affect the family?

_____

_____

_____

_____

_____

_____

_____

11 Unscramble each of the clue words. Copy the letters in the numbered cells to other cells with the same number.

ASRALY

					13

WEGA

			20

SENRU

24	6		22	30

RECHATE

14			4			

RIENFME

	9					

CODROT

31	10	5	25	3	18

LYAREW

29				16	17

HEACINMC

			15	27	2	12	

REVIDIARTX

8						23			

MERRAF

19	7				

FEARNHISM

	21	26	28		1	11		

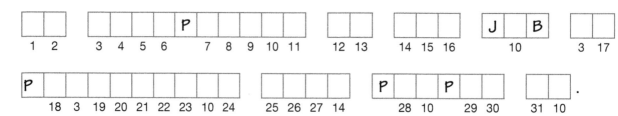

							P													J		B			
1	2		3	4	5	6		7	8	9	10	11		12	13		14	15	16		10			3	17

P															P		P				
	18	3	19	20	21	22	23	10	24		25	26	27	14		28	10		29	30		31	10 .

8 Fishing

Student's Book pages 106–111

1 Read pages 107 in the Student's Book. Use the maps of Antigua and Barbuda below to mark and label the main locations where fishermen can bring the fish they have caught to shore.

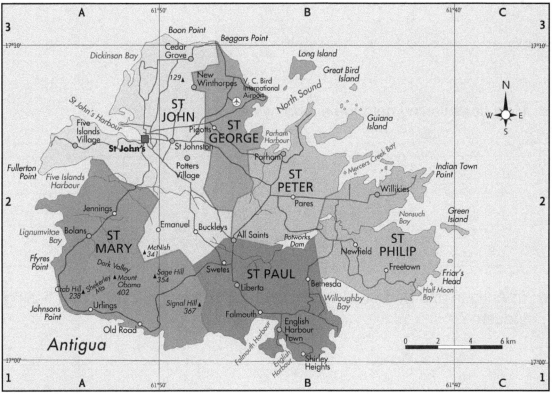

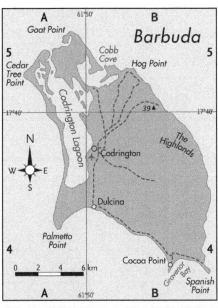

2 Read pages 106–107 in the Student's Book and answer these questions.

a In your own words, explain what fishing is.

_____

_____

b What is aquaculture?

_____

_____

c How does fishing help the economy of Antigua and Barbuda?

_____

_____

_____

_____

d In Antigua and Barbuda, how many people are employed in the fishing industry?

_____

_____

3 List the major fishing countries in:

a the Caribbean

_____

_____

b outside the Caribbean

_____

_____

4 Unscramble each of the clue words. Copy the letters in the numbered cells to other cells with the same number.

HINGIFS
| | | | | | | |
17 35 13 4 36

SEOTBLR
| | | | | | | |
 26   10

CHCON
| | | | | |
 21   28

TNE
| | | |
18 23

SARPT
| | | | |
33 25 14 11

PNSARPE
| | | | | | | |
3 16   29 30

RUGNT
| | | | | |
7   35

SAEF
| | | | |
15 1

AES
| | | |
38 12

PEDE
| | | | |
22

CABSU
| | | | | |
9

NEISORTUC
| | | | | | | | | |
32 24   19 2 37

DUYSINTR
| | | | | | | | |
5   27 20

SERIDASN
| | | | | | | | |
36 6

DARBAUB
| | | | | | | |
31   8

| | | | | | | | | | | | | | | | | | | | | | | | |
1 2 3 4 5 6 7   8 9 10 11   12 13   14   15 16 17 18 19 20

| | | | | | | | | | | | | | | | | | V | | | |
21 22 23   1 24 25   26 27 28 29 30   31 32 33 2   34 35 36 37 38

75

5 Use the internet to find a picture or diagram of a fishing method used in Antigua and Barbuda. Stick the picture below and then describe the method shown.

_____

_____

_____

_____

_____

_____

_____

_____

_____

_____

6 Find out the names of some fish caught in Antigua and Barbuda. Stick a picture and the name of each in the boxes below. Use the internet to help with this activity.

7 What is your favourite fish or fish product to eat, and why?

_____

_____

_____

8 Make a list of as many fish products as you can that are sold in shops and supermarkets.

_____

_____

_____

_____

9 Describe the process of canning a tuna fish.

_____

_____

_____

_____

_____

_____

10 Explain some of the problems which affect small-scale fishing in Antigua and Barbuda.

_____

_____

_____

Find words related to fishing in the wordsearch.

A	V	F	H	G	Z	V	R	O	L	D	B	E	S	W
I	H	Q	E	M	N	W	V	B	P	D	H	X	E	L
Z	Z	Z	F	K	T	I	I	L	M	E	Y	P	S	O
F	A	C	T	O	R	Y	H	E	N	E	M	O	R	Y
D	E	N	N	A	C	I	N	S	I	P	O	R	U	M
Y	R	E	N	I	H	C	A	M	I	R	N	T	N	Z
E	P	F	U	Z	Y	L	P	H	E	F	O	J	F	T
K	Z	G	R	E	J	O	I	T	O	J	C	T	L	R
W	V	E	U	E	R	G	S	A	W	B	E	X	S	P
P	R	U	E	T	S	B	R	S	W	A	T	E	R	A
N	K	C	T	R	O	H	T	O	S	F	A	V	K	K
J	Y	Q	Z	L	F	A	T	L	U	B	C	Q	R	I
Z	E	Q	S	F	O	U	C	R	N	P	I	H	A	Z
R	I	Y	J	B	P	T	L	T	V	E	E	G	N	I
J	N	J	B	O	E	W	M	X	J	V	A	R	F	D

boats   canned   deep   economy   export

factory   fishing   freeze   fresh   grouper

import   lobster   machinery   nurses

sea   water

9 Leadership

Student's Book pages 112–117

1 Use words from the box to fill in the gaps in the sentences below.

> authoritarian   democratic   government
>
> laissez-faire   leader   leadership   styles

a A _____ is someone who directs or leads a group of people.

b The act of leading people is referred to as _____.

c Leaders have different leadership _____.

d An _____ leader is one who makes all the decisions by themselves and then tells the members of the group what they should do and how they should do it.

e A _____ leader has discussions with group members any time a decision has to be made.

f A _____ leader gives all responsibility for decision-making to the members of the group.

g A _____ is a group of people who have the power and authority to make rules.

2 Write your own definition of each of the following terms.

a Leader

_____

b Leadership

_____

c Government

_____

d Authoritarian leader

_____

e Democratic leader

_____

f Laissez-faire leader

_____

g Democracy

_____

h Republic

_____

i Constitutional monarchy

_____

j Crown colony government

_____

3 Read the following scenarios. Choose the correct word from the box to fill in the blank and describe the scenario.

> **laissez-faire**   **authoritarian**   **democratic**

a John is the leader of the school's PTA. He told the members that they will

have three fundraising events over the next three months and identified

who will be in charge of events without having any discussions. John is an

_____ type of leader.

b Shana is the president of the All Saints Cricket Club. The club is planning

to have a fundraising event to raise money for an islandw tournament.

Shana sits with the team members and asks for ideas regarding the type

of fundraising. Shana is a _____ type of leader.

c Mary is in charge of planning a church service for the schools in her zone.

When the principals asked what items their respective schools should

contribute, Mary replied that they could do what they chose. Mary is a

_____ type of leader.

4 Read pages 114–115 in the Student's Book carefully and write T for true or F for false after each of the statements below.

a In Antigua, the government is chosen by the process of elections. _____

b In an election, people cast votes for the candidate of their choice. _____

c The candidate with the least votes wins. _____

d Antigua does not have a constitutional monarchy. _____

e The leader of a party usually becomes the Prime Minister. _____

f The winning candidate does not have a seat in parliament. _____

5 Write some of the services provided by the government for the people in the country in the diagram below.

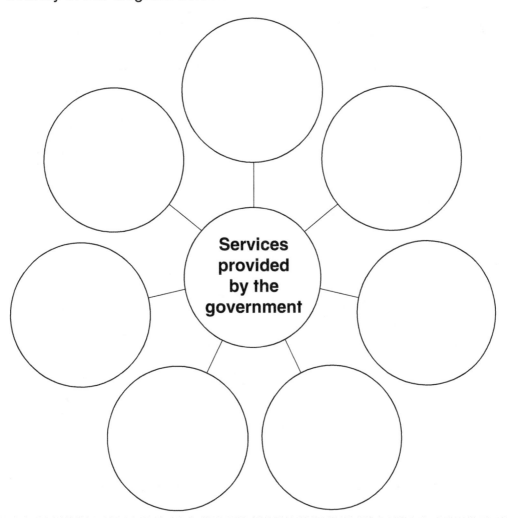

6 In each moneybag shown below, write one way in which the government of Antigua and Barbuda raises money to provide services to the people.

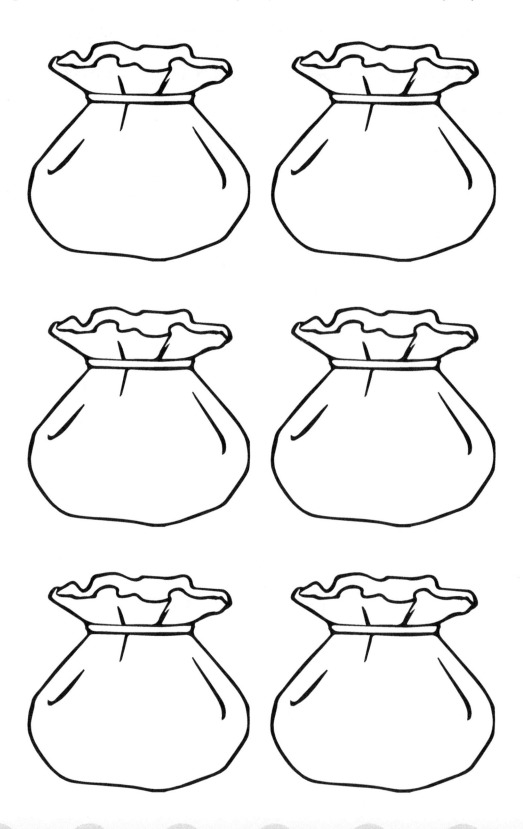

7 In your own words, explain why it is important for people to pay taxes.

_____

_____

_____

8 Use words from the box to fill in the blanks in the sentences below.

education	government	ministers
ministries	Technology	Works

a The Prime Minister of Antigua and Barbuda, who is the

head of the _____, creates

_____ that help with the provision of services.

He appoints _____ to be in charge of them.

b The Ministry of Education, Science and _____

in Antigua and Barbuda is responsible for providing

_____ from pre-school right up to

university level.

c The Ministry of _____ in Antigua and Barbuda

is responsible for making sure that the roads and government buildings

are kept properly.

9 Find words related to leadership in the wordsearch.

C	L	R	R	L	D	T	T	U	Y	O	S	I	P	M
O	P	K	E	T	Z	O	A	C	P	E	G	R	C	O
N	H	I	E	P	L	R	A	X	R	O	I	Y	I	N
S	S	Z	H	L	U	R	E	V	E	M	X	N	T	A
T	F	R	A	S	C	B	I	D	E	S	W	O	A	R
I	K	B	U	O	R	C	L	M	A	B	P	L	R	C
T	W	S	M	L	E	E	I	I	Z	E	D	O	C	H
U	Q	E	U	S	U	N	D	M	C	S	L	C	O	Y
T	D	M	K	W	I	D	O	A	H	G	E	F	M	I
I	G	A	Q	S	P	E	U	N	E	V	E	R	E	Z
O	E	Z	T	G	K	F	O	T	J	L	H	O	D	G
N	O	E	N	O	N	E	L	E	C	T	I	O	N	S
A	R	N	A	I	R	A	T	I	R	O	H	T	U	A
L	V	O	T	I	N	G	I	C	T	P	P	Z	A	E

authoritarian   ballot   colony   constitutional

democracy   democratic   elections   leader

leadership   monarchy   prime minister   republic

revenue   services   taxes   voting

Notes

Notes